Kindling

Talia Keyton

BookLeaf
Publishing

Presentation by *BookLeaf Publishing*

Web: www.bookleafpub.com

E-mail: info@bookleafpub.com

ISBN: 9789357615310

First edition 2022

To my past, present and future selves.

ACKNOWLEDGEMENT

To my love, N.J.C.

For your tender suggestions, your one-liners, your tolerance of my wild whirlwinds, and for carefully inspecting each one of my creations (no matter how ridiculous), upon request. Thank you for being the earth that holds my water.

PREFACE

This collection of poems is a reflection of existence in this realm through the strange mesh of my soul. They were gestated and birthed over the past two years as I worked through a very raw personal transformation during the process of scouting land on which to homestead.

It it my personal belief that in order to expand the human potential we must not fear the depths within ourselves or others. Rather, we must run towards the metaphorical bed of nails, mining the gold inherent within our negative emotions and the pain in our reality. I feel that authentic happiness lies in our ability to embrace our displacement, acknowledge our losses and gently seek beauty in the same.

I thank you for taking a journey with me through this poetic landscape of sorrows, longings and aspirations. It is my hope that you might arrive at the end as simply: yourself, and feel able to call it home.

Here.

I am here, because I want to be improbable.
Because I want to measure the weight of a closed loop.
I want to think on the truth of a forest,
be at the mercy of her cycles.
I want to be afraid of nothing, and to feel my strength
bolstered by the course of the path I pursue.
Living is so dear, especially when reduced
to its meanest terms.
How grateful I am
to be here.

Shackles

Shadow, dear love
your presence is felt
in the pit of my stomach;
a buckle-less belt.
My convictions may melt
but I see through your lies,
Shrewd Shadow, you're light.
Light spun demiguise.

Shame, oh sweet sister,
you've cast me downstream.
At the tide of a mind
now inversely esteemed.
How I scream to redeem,
but you're hogging the oar.
Allow flow, let it go.
See, we guide us to shore.

Fear, my old friend,
reared up like a snake.
You've tightened your coils
and demanded we quake.
Yes my bones they make shake,
but I see in your eyes
at the root of your nature
you're just love in disguise.

Email From a Friend

A glutton for affection's gaze,
two thirsty eyes drink up the words that
scatter the screen like a burst of birds
in a storm of song, without the singing.

Thrilled by loaded octaves, I beam
from far across the westward sea.
Scaling waves upon waves of thought debris
as time speaks with music's mouth.

My Ungulate

He surely is something.
To delight in a dame who loves
stale delicacies and art.
Amidst all seasons of the heart.
Her witchy winter, still spring
in his generous mind.

Before I go

A humming August heaven splits open,
spitting soft, sweet pearls of passion.
As above, so below.
Then the wind hurls hot sticky temptation
into arms spread wide with wreck-less longing.
Take a breath, make it slow.
And full lungs or wet hair are not enough
to capture this, before I go.

Phoenix

I know, you know who had the matches.
You know, I know who struck the sand.
At once, the victim and the arson.
We'll blaze together, hand in hand.

Distant Ones

Why recollection, are you half so lush
as the enchantment of proximity?

To the physically absent,
does your ethereality sense the weight
of my perpetual lean?

An infernal keel of false propinquity.
Iced only by the cool pack of memory.
A confusing sensibility
as the memories are warm,

reality cold.

Love Leaves

I woke to find it had become September.
Must have noticed the leaves rust,
dressing in red and gold for
their ephemeral waltz with fate.
I woke a little while later
to find you gone.

I miss all the sides of your soul.
I miss never licking that little mark
in the middle of your neck.

Be who you are? Even if it kills you.
As I know that I can, I know too that it will.
Over and over again, Even as I live.
Destined to rust. Like the leaves.

The Octopus

Here I am.
Sitting silently.
In the underbelly of a woman's sinking ship.
Hiding in the crust of years at sea;
forgotten debris of treasures past.
I try not to cry.

Up above,
An Octopus lurks.
Her many armed embrace
authoring alarum braille in oak.
Reading chaos in calm waters.

Ah, it could be so simple.

If only those arms were shorter.
If only one could stretch so far in faith
as to sink into the black velvet of the unknown.
I cry. Knowing I too must abandon ship.
I cannot sink for solidarity's sake.

Comfort's Captive

A noxious scent ocean;
tranquil fouling of motion.
She's a pool of still stagnant,
camouflaged as love potion.

Fear and Creativity

We share the same organs you see.
Creativity and me.
Forged in each other's fire,
we walk side by each; in mirrored echo.
deliberate duality for all of eternity.
And so it shall be.

2.5g of Golden Teacher

Just eat them.
Chew up and chase those
bitter sticks; they stoke internal kindling.
Ignited by the discharge of a slow spark
slinking home to it's filament.
She pseudo-sleeps.
In external dreams of baffled borders
and pinched, soggy margins
that melt on the tongue.

Send.

Sometimes I write to you.
Long laborious dates with Keyboard;
clack-flacking away at plastic,
slopping soul into imminent digi-space,
but never completely. Not neatly.
And always short something
with hook in finger,
I can never seem
to just press....

send.

The Violet Swallow Takes Risks.

His most treasured weapon: acceptance
for those who deal in absolutes.
For in deep dives of un-squandered freedom,
death can be flexible too.
Succumbing to gravity's authority,
as reality bends and perspective expands.
The violet swallow takes risks.

A Crocodile's Muse

Occulted violence always wears
a cloak of compassion; it seldom tears
for it's stitched up with virtue, a sinew of gold.
But this dragon is sick, and he won't be so bold
as to tell you the truth, to cast out the lies
or the years of deceit from a crown in disguise.

The scared and confused demand that we choose.
The rest cannot help but feel hopelessly used.
Til we've each walked a mile in the other side's shoes,
we'll be doomed to live life as a crocodile's muse.

Slither...

In moments of legless essence,
When my skin needs to die.
When, too hard, I've bitten down
on this tongue of bifurcated time.

It is then that I seek the sun
or else, sample the sky.
And sometimes...
sometimes I need only to slither

towards the comfort
                    of a poem.

She Belongs to all.

From the bottom of my heart and the seat of my soul,
I stand with you.
With your ancestors, whisked away from their birthright
by the morally blind.
With the innocent, returned to the Earth far too early
and shrouded in shadow.
At the hands of dogmatic demons,
on the word of an underground crown.
Claiming they were not everything
they turned out to be.
Everything they still are.
The "right to rule" belongs to no one.

When The Kibbles Run Out.

When the kibbles run out.
The short but stout seek tall and lanky.
Mongrels, wild with golden hue.

Beside the few scraggly, matted tails
(no longer waggly) pace newly purposed:
A lethal pack of chosen few.

The chosen seize us.
They sniff us out, no more to please us
with bites far worse than barks.

Humankind lacking forethought.
Mindless breeding, pleasure leading.
Our days are numbered,
when the kibbles run out.

The Poetic Impulse

To mine the gold of your soul:
wind up, and strike vein.
As the morphemes start streaming
in gilded chunks of unorganized aureate,
they are to be carefully considered.
Then lovingly reassembled,
until the sum of their parts gleam
in the afternoon sun of your spirit's eye.

The Key

Mind me, while you eat biscuits.
Mind me, when clouds form on the insides of your corneas.
Mind me, when you hear the latin names for animals.
Mind me, while you jest about the modern ethos.
Mind me, when you've peaked on mycelium;
fields of fantasy washing over you.
Mind me, when your certainty breeds insanity
and on heavy, humid nights when the bullfrogs croon.
Mind me at two o'clock in the morning
and then again at four.
Mind me, when someone fires off a warning shot,
then loads another.
Mind me, when crowds gather; a heartbeat through your feet,
feeling thousands as one.
Mind me, when firemen scurry like ants from a disturbed hill.
Mind my tone, timbre and tempo.
Mind me, when you think on magic. In those moments
between seconds at the back of the garden,
as you savour your last breath.

To Be a Bioform.

It is a potency
to simply exist.
In this skewed world
on a frosty morning.

After an earthly anguish,
It is miraculous all by itself
that one might still see
and seek beauty.

To embrace the alchemy of life
is hardest on the days I've had enough
of being brave about it: would rather
scream myself hoarse.

It has saved my spirit
to know; how to be idle
and that no matter how hard you hold on,

it's always over too soon.

Printed in the USA
CPSIA information can be obtained
at www.ICGtesting.com
LVHW050753050324
773584LV00003B/557

9 789357 615310